A Tale Of Two Mediaeval Chapels
In Lammana 'Parish' (Looe)

Dr Peter O. Leggat

Denise V. Leggat

ISBN 978-0-9929872-3-7

Printed and bound by Tradeprint.co.uk

Foreword

Since the last edition of *A Tale of Two Mediaeval Chapels in Lammana 'Parish' (Looe)* in 1998, a major archaeological excavation was carried out by Time Team in 2008. Although far from overshadowing the invaluable information presented in Dr. Leggat's booklet, it was felt necessary to update this work in light of new discoveries made on Looe Island, and the results of the excavations published by Wessex Archaeology in 2009. That update appears at the end of this reprinted edition in order to preserve the original text unaltered.

We would like to acknowledge our sincere gratitude to Mrs. Anne Robertson and Mrs. Jennifer Hodgson in giving us their kind permission to reprint the booklet in a new 3rd edition. We would also like to thank Lorraine Mepham, Senior Post Excavation Manager at Wessex Archaeology for permission to reproduce the diagram of trenches 1, 3 and 9 (Fig. 7) of the excavation site on Looe Island.

For those not already familiar with *A Tale of Two Mediaeval Chapels*, its content was impeccably researched over many years, as the copious notes, photographs and drawings in the Lammana archive testify; and both its co-authors worked tirelessly to present a highly informative booklet in an easy to read and enjoyable style.

The Editor
The Cornish Book Review
5th March, 2021

"We do not believe that the Glastonbury legends are records of facts; but the existence of those legends is a very great fact."

E.A. Freeman

Preface

We have to admit that the majority of the primary investigations have been accomplished by others. The results have been dispersed throughout a variety of publications. No sustained effort has been made to interpret, collate or assess them in an adequate historical context and bring them together in a continuous theme, highlighting the importance as to why the great and wealthy Benedictine Abbey of Glastonbury should have been so keen to maintain an ecclesiastical presence in a 'foreign' area in spite of local ecclesiastical opposition and even rancour.

The chronological relationship of the island chapel and its possible structure to that on the mainland has always been uncertain.

We believe we have been successful in clarifying these problems to some degree.

It would have been impossible to have undertaken a venture of this nature without help from many people. We have to thank the Royal Cornwall Museum for allowing us access to all C.K. Croft Andrew's field notebooks, correspondence files and original photographic records of the dig. In particular we received a major degree of assistance and advice from Anna Tyacke M.A. (Assistant Curator in Archaeology), also Brodrig Ross who made available to us his expert skill in copying original photographs and photographic artefacts held by the R.C.M. We are also indebted to the Librarian of the R.C.M., Angela Broome, for assistance in locating and copying documents relevant to the dig.

We were fortunate in that we were able to discuss the project in great detail with Dr. Lynette Olson, Senior Lecturer in History at the University of Sydney, whose advice was invaluable.

Locally we received every assistance possible from the officers of the Old Cornwall Society (Looe). The Minute Books and the Newspaper Cutting Books proved to be a virtual treasure trove of information. In particular we would like to mention F.E. Leese, Treasurer and Vice-President of the O.C.S. (Looe), who undertook the task of reading the original draft, and the late Doris Barker, the Secretary of the O.C.S. (Looe), who took a very active part in establishing a strong, forward-looking and continuing relationship with South Cornwall Heritage Coast Service. She was also responsible for the typing of the manuscript. Without the help of the above the whole project would have been stillborn.

Following the original excavations in 1935-1936, the site was allowed to revert to nature.

In Jubilee Year, 1977, Major Edward Kennington and his neighbours, Mr. & Mrs. Vic Hugo of Hannafore, cleared the whole of the site with great difficulty for the first time in five decades. Subsequently Caradon Council was persuaded to put an animal-proof fence around the site, but nothing was done to prevent the heavy re-growth of bramble, shrub and weeds once again obliterating all traces of the chapel foundations.

The site, in 1992, has now been successfully cleared by S.C.H.C.S. and this will be repeated as and when necessary. A sign post has been sited near to the east gable end of `Monk's House' and an excellent bench seat provided near the chapel on the mainland.

Extensive work by Lynette Olson and her colleagues in 1994 established the date of artefacts and in particular potsherds and glass fragments from the Lammana/Monks House sites, which has made a 2nd Edition of this booklet a necessity.

A weatherproof notice board with a synopsis of the history, a ground plan of the chapel remains and an artist's impression of the original building is sited near to the entrance stile.

We are indebted to Mr. & Mrs. D.A. Leslie and Mr. & Mrs. S.A.C. West for access to their gardens where, in 1941, C.K. Croft Andrew deposited carved stones from Lammana Chapel 'for safe keeping'.

P.O. Leggat

D. V. Leggat

(September 25th 1992)

1st Edition 1992
2nd Edition (Revised) 1998
3rd Edition (Reprint) 2021

The History

Once upon a time there was a very active religious community with a chapel on the Looe Island close to Looe in East Cornwall, and a second chapel on the foreshore immediately opposite the island serving a small 'Parish'. The whole belonged to the immensely wealthy Abbey of Glastonbury in Somerset from before 1144 to 1289. A great deal of confusion has arisen because both chapels have in the past been referred to as `Lammana', also the term 'island' in Cornwall can be used to refer to a piece of land girt by the sea or surrounded by other land.

Although Looe Island in the past, from the 13th century to the 17th century, has been referred to as 'Island of St. Michael of Lammana', 'Island of Lamagne', 'Island of St. George' and 'Looe Island', we will keep to the first title and to the name Chapel of St. Michael in regard to the island chapel. To avoid confusion we will refer to the chapel on the mainland as the Chapel of Lammana, although both were probably dedicated to St. Michael.

It would appear likely a small Priory was built on the mainland immediately North of the Lammana chapel. This, as indicated by Croft Andrew, lies under the farm road and the overburden of the field contiguous to the road and extending Northwards from the farm road. Concurrently the chapel of St. Michael was built on the Island and served by a causeway between 1085 and 1144. With the passage of time the causeway became unsafe with many casualties ensuing. In the 13th century it was decided to build a similar chapel dedicated to St. Michael on the mainland, and it was given the name Lammana. The building South East of the chapel, 'Monks House', was also constructed at the same time and probably served as a shelter and a refectory for the pilgrims.

There is a romantic history attached to the Island of St. Michael and Glastonbury Abbey. A legend persists that Joseph of Arimathea was a merchant trader following the old routes of the Phoenician tin traders, and that he brought the Christ Child to St. Michael's island and subsequently travelled himself to Glastonbury where he planted the Glastonbury Thorn that comes into flower in early January. The legend was preserved among the Celtic Welsh and probably came to Glastonbury in the latter part of the 12th century. It first came to the notice of a wider public when William of Malmesbury, a faithful servant of Glastonbury, mentioned it in his book '*De Antiquitate Glastoniensis Ecclesiae*'.

Glastonbury, like many mediaeval monasteries, was keen to promote itself through its possession of holy relics in order to attract pilgrims, whose visits brought considerable wealth and prestige. It is not surprising in these circumstances that the Abbey Authorities did everything in their power to encourage belief in the legend of Joseph of Arimathea. The 'cult of the Thorn' only became really popular towards the end of the 15th century. The present Thorn is descended from a cutting of the original, which was partially destroyed by a Puritanical zealot in the reign of Elizabeth I; the remains were totally destroyed by a Puritan during the Commonwealth when Oliver Cromwell was in charge of the destiny of the country.

There is evidence of Pre-Conquest occupation of the area from Hannafore Point to at least as far West as Lammana. A Bronze Age Funerary Urn was uncovered during the extension westward of a building development. A potsherd of Romano-Cornish origin was uncovered during building alterations to the Nailzie Point Hotel. Croft Andrew in the course of his excavations of Lammana chapel uncovered a collection of Romano-Cornish potsherds close to the exterior of the South wall of the chapel. It is possible these sherds were deposited during the building of the chapel and came with other debris from the area now occupied by the nave and the Chancel. These sherds have been dated to the 3rd Century A.D.

However, be that as it may, it is more than likely that St. Michael's Island was indeed a trading post in the pre-Christian era, and subsequently was a centre for Celtic Christianity, as were St. Michael's Mount off Lands End and Lundy Island in the Bristol Channel. The early Christian missionaries who came from Ireland, Wales and possibly Armorica in the 4th and 5th centuries may have felt the need of a safe base when attempting to convert the local inhabitants. However, this is supposition and until the chapel site on the Island is excavated it remains so.

There may be little to find on the island as the early Christian evangelical community would have had buildings of clay, wattle and thatch that would leave little evidence behind other than post holes and sherds of pottery. The later stone-built chapel would be a different matter.

It is very difficult to ascertain when the two chapels and the adjoining land came into the possession of Glastonbury. The Abbey rose to eminence in the 10th century with the appointment of Dunstan as Abbot. He subsequently became Archbishop of Canterbury and chief adviser to the King. It was under his care and influence that Glastonbury developed into a great and wealthy Benedictine foundation with a special relationship to the Throne, and also gained autonomy from the Bishop of Bath, which was to be a constant source, over the years, of strained relations.

King William I, towards the very end of his reign in 1085, arranged for a very detailed survey of all his possessions. He had replaced many of the Saxon Bishops and Abbots with his own Norman candidates and this included the Abbot of Glastonbury. There is no record of Lammana in the Domesday Book. It would be inconceivable that the very careful enquiries by his agent would have overlooked a property of this nature when assessing the worth of an important land-owning Abbey such as Glastonbury. Lammana must have come into possession of Glastonbury in the fifty-eight years between 1086 and 1144, when it was listed as one of the properties of the Abbey. In 1202 there was a partition of Abbey property with the Bishop of Bath and in the list of properties Lammana is again mentioned.

Hasculf de Soleigny, Lord of Porthlo (Port Looe) c. 1203, confirmed the grant of the 'whole island of St. Michael de Lammana with all its lands and tithes to Glastonbury Abbey which they hold by gift of my predecessors from ancient times'. He then goes on to make an additional grant of 'the tithes of Porthlo also rights of jurisdiction in the monk court and prohibition of interference in Lammana by the donor's bailiffs or servants'.

It is interesting to note in the opening statement that the chapel on the Island of St. Michael is regarded as the initial and more important of the two chapels. It is apparent from the above that the Island with its chapel and adjoining mainland property had already been administered de facto by Glastonbury for a considerable number of years, and the deed merely confirmed, added to and established the legal rights of the Abbey. The inference from the contents of the deed is the seniority of the island chapel to that on the mainland. The small group of monks was well regarded by the local community, and before 1230 Robert de Cardinham, Lord of the local manor of Trelawne, gave to Lammana 'one ferling of land with the timber rights in his woods'. However, not everybody was happy about their presence. Some local religious communities, and in particular Launceston Priory (Augustinian), were naturally jealous of this 'foreign' religious enclave in what they regarded as their sphere of influence.

In 1238 they laid claim to part of the tithes of Lammana. Neither party would give way and the problem was referred to the Pope. He referred the matter to a commission which decided: 'There were two buildings, the Chapel of St. Michael on the island and the Chapel of Lammana on the mainland'. The Commission awarded the tithes to the Priory of Launceston but it was directed to pay in compensation five solidi annually to the Abbey of Glastonbury. In 1245 Richard, Earl of Cornwall, stated 'all customs and dues belonging to him in respect of Lammana lands to go to the Abbot and Convent of Glastonbury on payment of ten solidi annually'. In 1279 Launceston surrendered all claims to tithes.

One would have thought that this would have been the end of the matter, but it was not to be. In 1290 a dispute arose between Walter de Treverbyn, the Patron, and the Prior of Launceston, which reached the Court of Common Pleas. The evidence of the Chapel's ownership was confused and it was directed that twelve jurors should come from the area to the court and give evidence of fact. They stated as follows: 'Lammana is a certain sea girt island in which a certain Chapel of St. Michael used to be kept up where the Abbots of Glastonbury, time out of mind, had monks celebrating Divine Service. Pilgrims often lost their lives in the stormy sea and a chapel to St. Michael was constructed on the mainland opposite the island'. In c.1289 Abbot John of Glastonbury, with the agreement of the King (Edward I), leased and then sold the land of Lammana with the two chapels and the Great Tithe, also the advowson, to the Lord of the Manor of Port Looe, Walter de Treverbyn. Thereafter the two now 'free chapels', with the attached land, remained under lay control until the Chantry Acts in the 16th century.

The patronage passed through two local families, the Dawnays and the Courtenays. The chapels in these circumstances could be regarded as manorial chapels. The function of the chapels was modified to some degree by establishing them as chantries. These are specialized chapels in which a priest is appointed whose sole duty is to say masses for a specific person. Prior and Suffragan Bishop John Vyvyan of Bodmin had little time for chantry priests. In 1538 he issued an edict: 'Chantry priests were to avoid idleness, were to teach children the Paternoster, the Creed, the Ten Commandments and the Seven Works of Mercy, in English or Cornish'. Lammana on the mainland was endowed by the Dawnay family in 1339 and a similar endowment was attached to the island chapel of St. Michael, probably in the early part of the 16th century, by the Courtenay family. Henry Courtenay, Marquis of Exeter, Earl of Devon, was executed in 1538. He was related through his mother to the King, but aspired too high, and had the misfortune to have an unreliable, hypochondriacal, Roman Catholic wife, and verbally incontinent servants, particularly William Kendall, who was little less than a freebooter and a rogue in Cornwall, disliked and feared by all who had dealings with him.

In relation to Lammana he is of some interest, as in c.1531 he is to be found in Looe, much to the annoyance of one of Henry VIII's Commissioners, John Amadas, currently investigating a case of piracy of a Breton boat off Looe. When challenged as to his presence in that place and at that time, William Kendall explained that he had come on the feast of St. George with his wife and one servant 'to view an image" in the Chapel of St. George. Possibly he was referring to the chapel on the Island of St. George (Looe island) but more likely to the Church of St. Mary in East Looe.

In 1548 Edward VI, son of Henry VIII, established a Commission to 'assess the assets of all religious establishments'. The assets of the two chapels were slight; Lammana had only 6 ozs. of plate and jewels. The chantry chapel of the island (St. Michael) had no jewels or vestments, and was rarely used for services. It is possible that the Commissioners of Henry VIII in 1538 during the suppression of the smaller monasteries had extended their activities to the manorial chapels. There is little in the way of information to help us to visualize the daily activities of the priest in charge, but in 1548 there is a record that there were sixty parishioners that attended the chapel on the mainland intermittently, coming from Portbyhan (West Looe), Port-looe and Hannafore. The Chantry Priest was required to celebrate communion five times a year. In his absence the curate from Talland Church took over.

Following the Chantry Acts of 1547 and in 1548 it is likely that there was a progressive reduction in the use of the chapel by the local community. In c.1550 there is a recorded deed of sale, by presumably the current patron of the living, who had not exercised his right of appointing an incumbent for a considerable number of years, with Thomas Bell of Gloucester, Knight, and Richard Duke of London Esq. 'Grant to the aforesaid: 1) the island of Lamane Cornwall within the Parish of Talland and the chapel and land pertaining to that island, and 2) the late free chapel or chantry within the island of Lamane for the sum of £1297 10s.' (Here the document is referring to the

16

chapel on the mainland in the 'Parish' of Lamane, entirely surrounded by the lands of the Parish of Talland and is therefore a 'land island'. The 'Parish' of Lamane is strictly speaking not a true Parish but as it has in the past been referred to as a 'Parish' by several authors we have continued to do so).

Thereafter the chapel disappears from historical record until 1727 when the Vicar of Talland, Richard Doige, supported by two churchwardens and thirteen principal inhabitants, replied to a series of questions as follows: 'The Parish of Lamane is part of the Parish of Talland, consisting of the Barton of Port Looe and one other tenement and about half the borough of West Looe, but as to when it was incorporated no trace can be found. The Vicar of Talland received no tithes from it but the lay owner (impropriator) paid a charge of £4 per annum to the priest in charge. The ruins of the chapel on the mainland are still apparent'. The measurements are given.

In 1815 Thomas Bond inspected and measured the remains of the chapel on the mainland. In neither of the above do the measurements match up with those of Croft Andrew following his excavations in 1935/36. Many potsherds and fragments of glass vessels, assigned to the 16th and 17th Century, were found in Lammana chapel. These all belonged to domestic vessels which would suggest the building was, at that time, being used as a domestic dwelling.

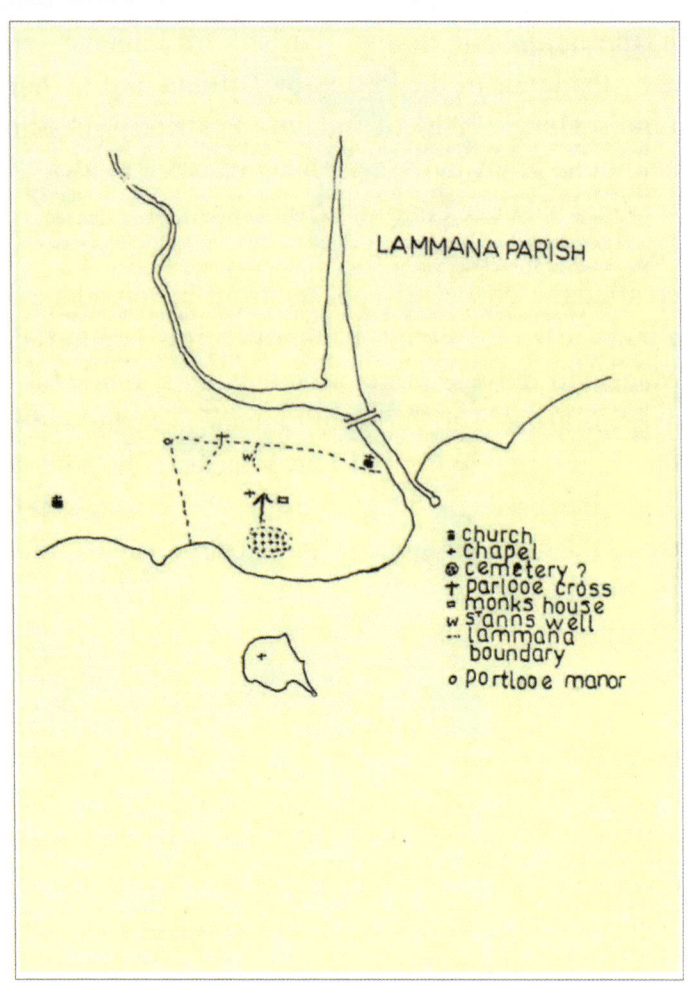

LAMMANA PARISH

- church
- chapel
- cemetery ?
- parlooe cross
- monks house
- s'anns well
- lammana boundary
- Portlooe manor

Diagram of Lammana Parish (© Peter Leggat)

The "Parish"

This was small, about 21.26 hectares including the island, but of course the original religious foundation, a Priory, probably never had more than three to four brothers as a maximum at any one time. The boundaries of the 'parish' on the mainland are: on the east side, the road from the waterfront, up West Looe hill to the first `T' junction; there it turns south to Portlooe and thence down the side of a small stream, to meet the sea close to Portnadler at Old Mills. The parish also includes the sea shore and cliffs from Old Mills to Looe harbour excluding the church of St. Nicholas and its immediate environment.

As noted above, part of West Looe (Portbyhan) and two small hamlets, Portloe and Hannafore, were included in the 'parish'. There is a well, the Well of St. Ann, to be found on the right hand side of Well Lane, which comes off on the left hand side, halfway up West Looe Hill. It is possible that this might have been used by the monks of the small Priory on the mainland, but they also had the facility of the spring at Portlooe Barton if they so wished.

At the top of West Looe Hill on the left side is a small lane belonging to a farm. Where it leaves West Looe hill a small round-headed Celtic Cross is set into the hedge. The cross was 'rescued' by the Looe Old Cornwall Society in 1930 from a local farm, where it had probably been used as a mowstead in the mowhay. These are granite "toadstools" placed under hay and straw ricks throughout Cornwall to keep the ricks free of ground moisture and vermin. The dimensions of the Cross are as follows: 1.1m overall with a head originally rounded, and about 33 cms in diameter. A shallow cross has been chiseled in the shaft and head of the Celtic

Cross. This, though badly worn, is still visible. It was decided by the Society to set it up in its present position because it was the site of a previous boundary cross, now missing, known as Parlooe Cross.

The Portlooe Cross (© Peter Leggat)

There is a tradition that a mediaeval burial ground is yet to be excavated on the relatively flat bit of ground between the site of Lammana Chapel on the mainland and the cliff edge. H.K. Lewis, sometime Rector of Talland, states that 'In the past coffin rings have been found in the above area'. However, during the excavation by Croft Andrew, burials were identified in the chancel area. Lynette Olson was of the opinion that the chancel could have been built on part of a mediaeval graveyard extending eastwards from the chancel. We agree with this suggestion.

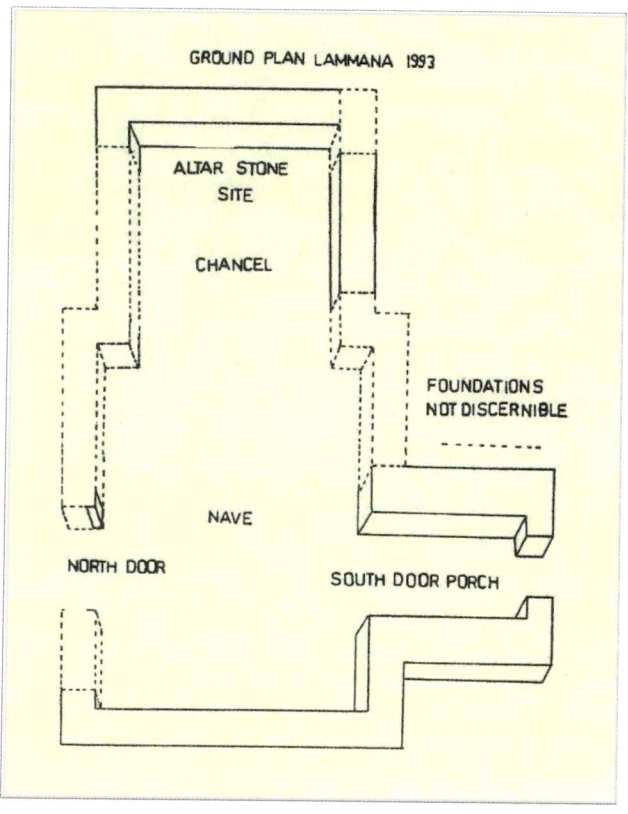

Ground plan of Lammana 1993 (© Peter Leggat)

The Excavation

The site of the chapel on the mainland remained in considerable doubt until a series of excavations were undertaken by Mr. C.K. Croft Andrew and Rev. H.A. Lewis in 1935/36. We owe a great debt to these gentlemen who were very active members of the Old Cornwall Society for a considerable number of years. The former was at one time chairman of the Society when it was founded in 1927 and held the office of Recorder from 1927 to 1931. Both were very active in researching the history of the two chapels and in locating the site of the chapel on the mainland, which is still not recorded on the current Ordnance Survey maps.

The whole of the coastal area from Hannafore point to Old Mills is of pre-Christian religious significance as, at a date unknown but prior to 1934, members of the O.C.S. (Looe) were shown an urn containing fragments of cremated bone in the possession of the Rector of Landulph, with a history that it had been unearthed while digging the foundations of a house at Hannafore. In 1941 C.K. Croft Andrew referred to a 'Bronze Age urn c.800 B.C.' discovered during building operations at Hannafore in 1912. It was in 1929 that C.K. Croft Andrew drew the attention of the Old Cornwall Society (Looe) to the importance of the site and suggested that it should be excavated using volunteer diggers. Another six years were to elapse before excavation started. Even then funds and labour were minimal and it is impressive that he achieved so much with so little before funds ran out. He started by excavating the main chapel, which proved to be a rectangular building. It was built into the hillside and because of the physical restrictions of the area it was set 20° out of true in relation to a true East/West axis.

Remains of Lammana Chapel 1993 (© Peter Leggat)

In the main the stone work was native mudstone (killas). This is a rather soft stone. The door jambs and lintels were hard slate. The slabs of mudstone were laid horizontally without mortar on clayey earth. Mortar was subsequently used in repairing the upper walls, roof, doorways and, in lieu of plaster, upon the interior faces of the walls. Mid-way along and facing each other are a North door and a South door with a porch. There was another smaller door at the North East corner of the nave, 76.2 cms wide, leading into a 1.2m wide passage plastered internally and leading eastwards. In view of the plasterwork, this was possibly covered when in its original state. The North door opened into a flight of steps which ascended in a gentle curve towards (?) a further set of domestic buildings covered by overburden. Croft Andrew did not have the labour and funds to remove the above, but he was of the opinion that cloisters lay immediately to the north of the Chapel.

The building was divided into a fairly large nave and a small chancel. The nave was 8.3m x 4.6m; the chancel 3.4m x 4.0m. These measurements are taken internally. The South East corner of the chancel was difficult to delineate as the ground sloped fairly steeply and had to be built up but had suffered excessively from the weather and the trauma of the years. The thickness of the walls varies between 81.3 cms and 91.4 cms. The width of the north and south doors is 1.2m. In the nave there are stone built benches around the wall footings. This is a similar arrangement to that found in Madron Baptistry. The nave communicates with the chancel through an opening of 1.8m. The chancel was paved with stone slabs. The walls were plastered internally with mortar. Croft Andrew indicates in his field notes that there was part of an 'altar stone' close to the east wall of the chancel, 1.5 m by 91.4 cms, with painted plaster on its north facing wall. Similar areas of painted plaster were found on the chancel walls and also areas of whitewash. An oblong block of native slate (a lintel?) was located near the north door, and a possible jamb stone with an angled end was near the south door.

In the South East corner of the nave and the adjacent chancel three burials were unearthed. The remains were facing east and were not in coffins. Croft Andrew was of the opinion that the nave was probably pre-Norman, the chancel 12th or 13th century, and both large north and south doors 15th century. He leaned to possibly prior to 700 A.D. for the date of the Nave. The evidence is more in favour of the original building being mediaeval: late 11th to mid-12th Century.

Lammana Excavations in 1936
looking towards the South door

Many of the potsherds discovered on the Lammana site were from domestic objects some of which were identified as cooking pots and bowls belonging to the 13th Century.

The chapel on the island existed long before the chapel of Lammana, which is probably a copy. It is so far unexcavated [1] and may indeed demonstrate evidence of its early Celtic Christian origins. Islands such as Lundy in the Bristol Channel, St. Michael's Mount and many others, particularly off the coasts of Scotland and Ireland, were favoured sites for the establishment of such communities.

[1] See Appendix 1

South doorway looking towards the Island (© Peter Leggat)

During the excavations a variety of artefacts were unearthed: a number of square and oblong stones with a re-entrant angle at one corner which are parts of door jambs associated with the south door, hand-made unglazed ridge tiles with a possible dating of the 13th century, a variety of rough-hewn slabs from local slate of various colours, a few lighter and better cut slates and tiles. Many of the above had holes for wooden pegs. Some of the slabs and tiles still had mortar attached to them. The roof of the chapel must have been mended many times throughout the ages and it obviously had the appearance of a patchwork quilt.

The doorjambs for the south door were vertical with a recessed edge for the door, and a round arch. Parts of stone mullions were discovered. It is possible that they belonged to a window with two lights in the east wall of the chancel.

Below the modern topsoil the whole area was strewn with

debris from the demolition of the original building. There were numerous sherds of domestic pottery of several periods within the Middle Ages, some unglazed and others glazed. A single intact food pot was discovered, fashioned by hand and not on a potter's wheel. This has since gone missing. There were also many sherds of glass, both clear and coloured. Some of these have been provisionally identified is belonging to 16th and 17th century domestic articles.

To the east of Lammana Chapel, 150m, is to be found the gable end of a mediaeval building inserted in a boundary wall, with the typical narrow splayed windows of the period. A certain amount of unorganized digging had taken place in the immediate east side of this structure in (?) the first two decades of the 20th century, and while digging the foundations of a suburban house east of the gable end 'a wall was found three feet below the surface at right angles to the existing wall and also a millstone'. It may have been part of the mediaeval building. Mills were very common in this part of Cornwall. Every village had one. In the 17th century a mill which went by the name of Parlooe Mill was to be found in the Old Mills area on the western boundary of Lammana 'Parish'. It is possible that the millstone originated there.

Croft Andrew and his associates were anxious to excavate a putative building west of the gable end, but funds were running low and we suspect a time factor was becoming important, as it is apparent that Croft Andrew had many calls on his archaeological skills. It was decided to drive three trial trenches. The foundations of a large building were exposed. The internal measurements were 16.8m x 8m, divided into three rooms by a longitudinal and a transverse partition.

Transverse trench 9 ft. from the field wall, Lammana 1936

The few potsherds discovered belonged to the 13th century. The east gable end was also attributed to the same date. In 1943 Croft Andrew deposited, for safe keeping, a variety of stone work with several residents of Looe. He presumably filled in the greater part of the excavations in the Lammana Chapel/Monks House area. Today there is no sign of an 'altar stone' or stone door lintels. Lynette Olson about six years ago located a carved stone (? a mullion) in a local garden, the owners were quite unaware of its significance. In 1992 we found other stones in another local garden. We have a strong suspicion that there are others yet to be uncovered. The (?mullion) was deposited with the Royal Cornwall Museum, to join a variety of carved stones and many artifacts from the Lammana site; also Croft Andrew's note books, drawings and site diagrams in addition to his correspondence file.

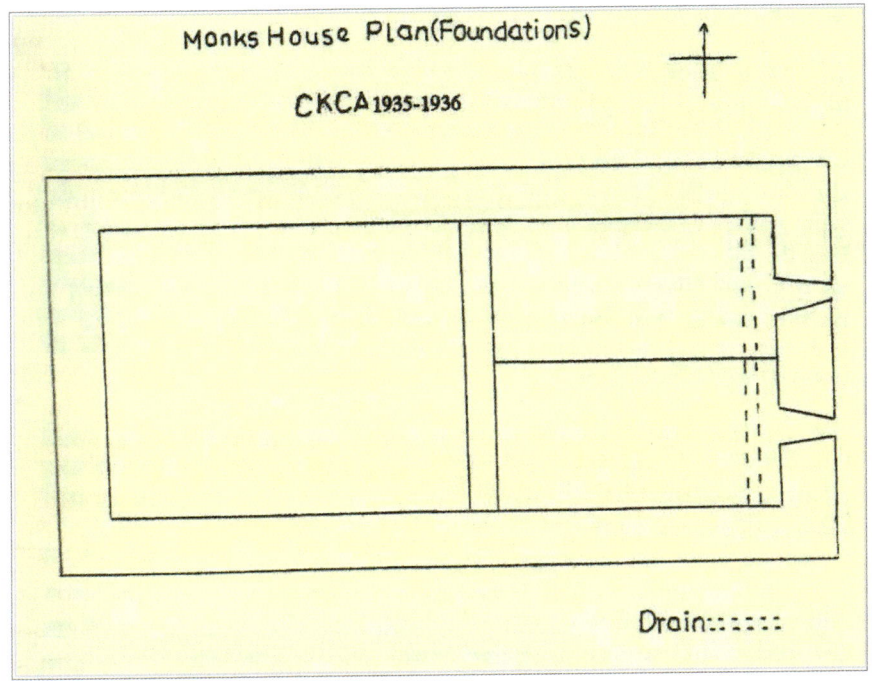

Monk's House Plan Foundations – CKCA 1935-1936 (© Peter Leggat)

The Island Chapel and Monk's House

There is every likelihood that the chapel on the island is mediaeval in origin like its mainland twin.

There is also a strong possibility that it was preceded by a Celtic Christian foundation and before that (Druidical?) as there is evidence of Bronze Age urn burial in the adjacent mainland area. The evidence of Celtic Christian activity is by comparison and inference. Lundy Island and St. Michael's Mount are both associated with the Celtic Christian church.

It is worthwhile considering the nature of the name Lammana, also known as Lamayne, Lamene and Laman. The prefix 'Lan' points to one of the little Celtic monasteries or eremitical enclosures which preceded our parish churches, and refers to the round enclosure within which were to be found the beehive-shaped dwelling places of wattle and clay, later of stone, of the monks. The 'Lan' also enclosed the small church and the cemetery. The translation of the suffix is less certain. Croft Andrew was of the opinion that it could be translated as 'stone'. and hence it would refer to the 'stone Lan' or stone church.

It is much more difficult to imagine the nature of the Chapel of St. Michael on the island. A 16th century map of the coast between Fowey and Looe includes the island of St. Michael (Looe) and a sketch map of a chapel on the North West end of the island. It is a rectangle in shape, with a roof that has a fairly steep pitch. There is a tall door with a round arch at one end, and in the gable end above the apex of the gable is a Latin Cross. Some distance away from the apex of its twin is the upper end of a flagstaff with a square flag. There are two small oblong windows in the side wall. Allowing for artistic licence it probably has the main features of the original chapel. There is no knowledge as to its age, but early mediaeval is the most likely, fashioned to some degree on an earlier Celtic Christian church.

In 1860 the island was visited by Mr. & Mrs. John Vague who noted 'Chapel remains obvious'. In 1932 Croft Andrew visited the island and commented 'on the crest of the island stood a second chapel of which the only relics are a few cut stones'.

In 1981 Professor A.C. Thomas located the site of the chapel and noted: 'site overgrown, no building plan can be distinguished, but there were on the site two well carved fragments of engaged columns in fine grained sandstone. What was even more interesting, a shard from an amphora originating in the Aegean Region'. A visit to the island in 1992 confirmed that the chapel site with the sandstone columns was unchanged.

There was a small Priory close to Lammana in association with the two chapels. It was never served by more than three Benedictine monks, although one was designated as Prior. It is decidedly odd that a large and wealthy Abbey such as Glastonbury should be prepared to retain and service for about 184 years such a small ecclesiastical unit, in spite of determined efforts by Launceston Priory to take it over. Glastonbury must have held it in high regard, probably because of its association with the legend of Joseph of Arimathea, which Glastonbury was very keen to promote on all occasions. The Abbey was a great place for relics of all kinds, and William of Malmesbury in 1120 had this to say of it: 'The church is certainly the oldest I am acquainted with in England. In it are preserved the remains of many saints, nor is any corner of the church destitute of the ashes of the holy. The very floor inlaid with polished stones and the sides of the altar itself above and beneath are laden with a multitude of relics'.

If Croft Andrew's supposition in regard to cloister and domestic monastery buildings north of the chapel is correct, then a use must be suggested for the very large building 150m east of the chapel, today referred to as 'Monks House'. It may be of some help to consider the old place names east of the Priory. The area east of the boundary wall, and now occupied by private dwellings, was known as White Cross, and another now occupied by the municipal tennis court was previously known as Crows Sans (Cross Sands). This is quite close to the Coastguard Station, in front of which is to be found a natural fault in the rocks, in which is a spit of sand which extends more than halfway to the island.

Directional crosses have been common in Cornwall for many hundreds of years. It would appear at least plausible for a high cross to indicate the commencement of the way to the island when the tide and weather permitted. In these circumstances the holy brothers in the small Priory would be there to service the pilgrims, and the relatively large so-called 'Monks House' would provide dormitory and refectory facilities for pilgrims.

There still remains a folk memory of the religious importance of Looe Island in that until very recently it used to be the custom to try to cross dry shod to the island on a suitable ebb spring tide closest to Good Friday.

Looe Island – Ebb Spring tide 1992 (© Peter Leggat)

APPENDIX

In January 2008, at the invitation of the Cornwall Wildlife Trust researchers from Channel 4's TV show, Time Team, visited the mainland chapel site at Hannafore, West Looe. Due to bad weather they were prevented from examining the chapel site on Looe Island. Wessex Archaeology were commissioned by Videotext Communications Ltd to record archaeological finds during the making of the programme, and to evaluate the archaeological context of the three sites associated with the conventual buildings of the Priory of Lammana. What follows is a summary of Wessex Archaeology's *Evaluation and Assessment Results*, published in February 2009.

Post archaeological assessment

The evaluation concluded that there was 'no definitive evidence for prehistoric activity on either site.' [2]

Looe Island

On Looe Island, a large stone buried in the grounds of Island House 'may have been prehistoric,' but the absence of a socket indicated that it had been removed from another location on the island, probably during 19th century landscaping. Romano-British (AD 43 – 410) pottery was found in two ditches, and a small hoard of eight Roman coins dating between AD 253 and 330. Since no modern investigation had been

[2] Wessex Archaeology, *Looe, Cornwall: Archaeological Evaluation and Assessment Results*, 2009, p. iii

carried out of the island chapel, the excavations led by field archaeologist Phil Harding, confirmed that the ruins were those of the former mediaeval chapel; a two cell building consisting of a nave and chancel.

Orientation of the island chapel facing north east

The construction of the chapel was that of a single phase with the addition of a large buttress to the south west corner of the nave in the 13th century. An inhumation grave was found underneath the area of the chancel arch, and showed evidence of being disturbed; probably due to antiquarian activity on the island in the latter part of the 18th century. A second burial lay outside the southern wall of the chapel possibly a cist grave consisting of flat stones arranged vertically on four sides to form a container, with larger flat stones placed across the top to form a lid. The *Evaluation and Assessment Results* stated that neither of these burials were investigated any further, nor could they be securely dated. The only dating evidence available was pottery in the upper fill of the inhumation grave in the chancel, possibly 15th or 16th century.

35

The results of Croft Andrew's excavations of the mid 1930s were re-evaluated in 1994 by Dr Lynette Olson, senior lecturer of History at Sydney University, along with Cathy O'Mahoney, Ann Preston-Jones and Peter Rose. [3] Wessex Archaeology were able to confirm Croft Andrew's ground plan of the mainland chapel as reproduced by Dr Olson. [4]

The chapel consisted of a nave and chancel with a south facing porch, and a second entrance to the north of the building. Professor Nicholas Orme of Exeter University has described the *porch* as the threshold to a sacred place, bringing people from 'out of secular life into the arms of Holy Church.' [5] Inside the porch would have been a stoup containing holy water, which the parishioners used to sanctify themselves as they entered into the nave.

There was some evidence to suggest the presence of a rood screen in front of the chancel arch. The rood screen separated the nave from the chancel. The chancel, which was the responsibility of the priest or chaplain to maintain, was regarded as a sacred space holier than the nave; the latter being the responsibility of the laity. Access to the chancel through the rood screen was limited to the priest, except for marriages, and patrons of the chapel; usually the lords of the manor at Portlooe up

---

[3] *Lammana, West Looe; C.K. Croft Andrew's excavations of the chapel and Monks House, 1935-6*, Cornish Archaeology No. 33, 1994, pp. 96-129
[4] Olson, et. al., p. 100
[5] Nicholas Orme, *Cornwall and the Cross*, Christianity 500 – 1560, Phillimore, 2007, p. 102

until 1549. [6] One inhumation burial *in situ* was found under the chancel floor, along with indications of two other possible graves, and a stone lined reliquary.

South facing porch prior to excavation in 2008

A radio carbon date of a humerus (arm bone) taken from the inhumation burial under the chancel floor, gave a date range of between AD 1200-1280. The skeleton was probably that of an adult male between 35-55 years old, with an approximate height of 5 feet 4 ½ inches tall. Burials under chancel floors of churches or chapels are usually associated with people of high ranking status, such as the patrons or founders of the church, or important members of the clergy.

[6] Charles Henderson, *The Cornish Church Guide*, Oscar Blackford, 1925, p. 201

Inhumation burial under the chancel floor, mainland chapel

Archaeologists Jackie McKinley and Brigid Gallagher unearthed a reliquary in the chancel area near the burial. Constructed of flat stones in the same way as a cist grave, reliquaries usually contained religious items regarded as too precious to display inside the church such as holy relics; or sometimes the bones of someone important associated with the foundation of the site.

The overall conclusion reached by Wessex Archaeology was that the 'foundation date of the Lammana Chapel remains unknown.' [7] However, their caveat to this statement, (based on all the available evidence), is that it is unlikely to pre-date the Norman Conquest; and that

[7] Wessex Archaeology, p. iii

along with the previous evaluation undertaken in 1994, suggest that the chapel 'is likely to have been 12th century in origin.' [8]

Artists impression of a reliquary

Afterword

When Lammana was sold to Ralph Bloyhou in 1289, he was acting on behalf of Walter de Treverbyn, the lord of the manor of Portlooe. When Sir Walter tried to present Andrew as the new rector, [9] a former abbot of Launceston Priory appealed to the bishop of Exeter that the advowson was rightfully theirs. The bishop refused the presentation and Sir Walter brought a royal writ *quare impedit* against the former prior. [10] The writ commenced a common law action in the Court of

[8] Wessex Archaeology, p. iii; see also Olson, et. al., p. 125
[9] The former rector was the abbot of Glastonbury, John of Taunton
[10] P.L. Hull, *The Cartulary of Launceston Priory*, (Lambeth Palace MS. 179), Devon & Cornwall Record Society, 1987, 167-8

Common Pleas at Westminster to decide the disputed right of the presentation of Andrew the priest, and more importantly, the advowson of Lammana. Sir Walter successfully obtained the writ in November 1289 and sued Launceston Priory for damages of £40. Eleven months later after the Sheriff of Cornwall had been instructed by the Court to form a jury of twelve local men, the verdict was given in favour of Sir Walter.

In giving their evidence to the court, the jurors had stated that due to 'the stormy seas, a certain chapel of Saint Michael was constructed upon the coast opposite the said island.' However, this may not have been be a literal 'construction,' as many churches and monasteries were said to have been founded where an earlier establishment was known to exist. It is feasible that Glastonbury appropriated the chapel around 1144, and after refurbishing it with the addition of a chancel, rededicated it to St Michael the Archangel.

Discussing the mainland chapel in the early 1980s, Martin Picken, a leading authority on mediaeval Cornwall, suggested that: 'It is, however, difficult to believe that the great Somersetshire abbey would have undertaken the maintenance of so small, remote and inconvenient a property as Lammana in Cornwall unless it was already the focus of a local cult of some distinction; and that would predicate the presence of a chapel there.' [11]

---

[11] 'Light on Lammana,' *Devon and Cornwall Notes & Queries*, 35, 1982-6, pp. 281-6; in *A Medieval Cornish Miscellany*, by W.M.M., Picken, ed. O.J. Padel, Phillimore, 2000, p, 71.

Artist impression of the mainland Chapel of St Michael
of Lammana after the addition of the chancel

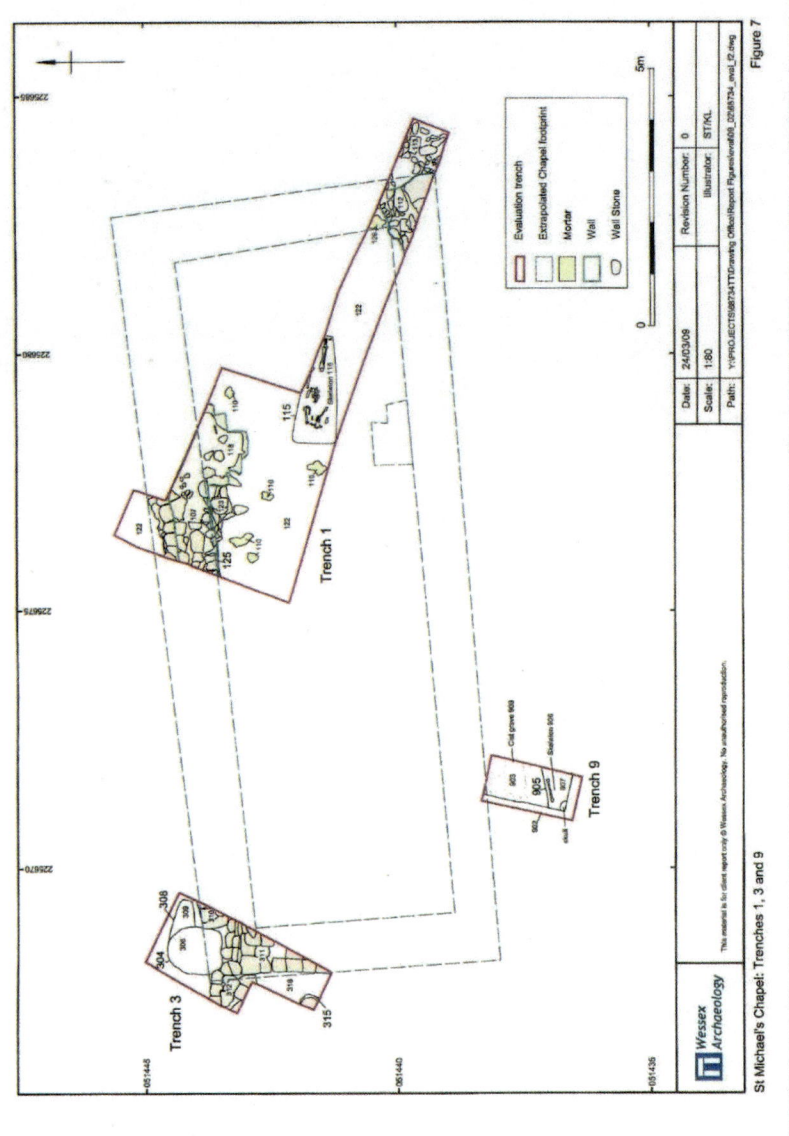

Excavation trenches on Looe Island, 2008
(Source: Wessex Archaeology)

References

Andrew, C.K., *Maina Parc (the Monk's Field)*, Western Morning News, 27th September 1932

Andrew, C. K., *Lammana (Nr. Looe)*, Devon and Cornwall Notes and Queries 19, p.145, 1936

Ashe, G., *King Arthur's Avalon (the Story of Glastonbury)*, Collins (London) 1957

Atkins, E., *We Bought an Island*, G.G. Harrap Ltd., 1976

Atkins, E., *Tales from our Cornish Island*, G.G. Harrap Ltd., 1986

Branigan, K. and Fowler, P.F. (ed), *The End of the Roman South West*, pp 198-213, Newton Abbot, 1976

Carter, G., *Outlines of English History*, Ward Lock, London, 1984

Gascoigne, J., 17th Century Map of Cornwall, pub. Devon & Cornwall (Record) Soc., 1991

Henderson, C., *"East Cornwall"* – unpublished manuscript, Royal Institute of Cornwall Library

Hencken, H.O., *The Archaeology of Cornwall and Scilly*, (London), 1932

Keast, John, *History of East and West Looe*, Phillimore & Co Ltd (Chichester) Sussex, 1987

Laing, I., *The Archaeology of Late Celtic Britain and Ireland, (c.400-1200)*, London, 1975

Lewis, H.A. (Rev), *The Child Christ at Lammana*, 1936

Lysons, D. (Rev.), Magna Britannia, Vol 3, pp. 108-109, 16th Century Map, Island of St. Michael, T. Caldwell & W. Davies, London, 1814 [Cotton MS Augustus I i 38, c. 1539]

Lyte, M.C.H. (ed), *Calendar of the Patent Rolls*, Public Records Office, Edward VI 1547-1553 (6 vols), London, 1924-1929

Old Cornwall Society, Looe, Minute Book 1927-1946, Newspaper Cutting Book 1931, Recorder Book 1933-1939

Olson, L., *Studies in Celtic History XI, Early Monasteries in Cornwall*, Boydell Press, Woodbridge, 1989

Olson, L, et al, *C.K. Croft Andrew's 1935 and 1936 Excavations of Lammana Chapel and Monks House*, Cornwall Archaeology, Vol. 33, 1994

Orme, N. (ed), *Unity and Variety, A History of the Churches in Devon and Cornwall*, University of Exeter Press, 1991

Padel, O.J., *Cornish Place Names*, Alison Hodge, Penzance, 1988

Paynter, W.H., *Looe, A History and Guide*, Parade Printing Works, Plymouth, 1970

Paynter, W.H., *A Relic of Ancient Christianity, Chapel ruins at Hannafore*, Cornish Times, 18th February, 1972

Peter, T.C., *St. Piran's Old Church*, Journal of the Royal Institute of Cornwall XVI, pp. 133-143 1904-1906

Picken, W.M.M., *Light on Lammana*, Devon and Cornwall Notes and Queries, pp. 281-286, 1985

Radford, C.A.R. & Ashe, G. (ed), *The Quest for Arthur's Britain*, pp. 75-100, London, 1968

Rowse. A.L., *Tudor Cornwall*, Jonathan Cape, London 1941

Snell, L.S., *Documents towards a history of the Reformation in Cornwall No. 1., Chantry Certificates for Cornwall*, Townsend, 1953

Taylor, T., *The Celtic Christianity of Cornwall, Divers Sketches and Studies*, pp. 104-121, Longman Green, London, 1916

Thomas, C., *Gwithian, Ten years work (1949-1958)*, West Cornwall Field Club, Camborne, 1958

Thomas C., *Post Roman rectangular house plans in the South West, Some suggested origins*. Proceedings of the West Cornwall Field Club M.S.G., (1956-1961)156-61

Thomas. C., *The Early Christian Archaeology of North Britain*, Oxford University Press, London, 1971

Thorn, Caroline& Frank (ed), *Domesday Book* (Section on Cornwall), Phillimore, Chichester, 1979

Western Morning News and Daily Gazette *"Olden Days in Cornwall, buried remains of a Chapel"* September 1936